A PLACE IN
HISTORY

...E
...ANDY
...CHES

...ILLIAMS

...N WATTS
...SYDNEY

First published in 2010 by Franklin Watts

Franklin Watts
338 Euston Road
London NW1 3BH

Franklin Watts Australia
Level 17/207 Kent Street, Sydney, NSW 2000

Produced by Arcturus Publishing Limited,
26/27 Bickels Yard, 151–153 Bermondsey Street,
London SE1 3HA

Series concept: Alex Woolf
Editor and picture research: Alex Woolf
Designer: Phipps Design

Picture credits:
Archives Normandie 1939–1945: 28.
Arcturus: 10 (Stefan Chabluk), 33 (TMS), 38 (TMS).
Corbis: 9 (Bettmann), 15 (Jacques Langevin/Sygma), 19 (Bettmann), 20 (Bettmann),
29 (Bettmann), 39 (Hulton Deutsch Collection), 40 (Bettmann), 41 (Bettmann),
42–43 (Peter Turnley).
Getty Images: cover *background* (Time & Life Pictures), cover *foreground* (Time & Life
Pictures), 6–7 (US Army/Time & Life Pictures), 8 (Keystone/Hulton Archive), 11 (LAPI/
Roger Viollet), 12 (Galerie Bilderwelt/Hulton Archive), 14 (Keystone/Hulton Archive),
18 (AFP), 22 (Apic/Hulton Archive), 23 (Popperfoto), 24 (Popperfoto), 26 (Popperfoto),
27 (Frank Scherschel/Time & Life Pictures), 31 (Paul Popper/Popperfoto), 32 (Popperfoto),
34 (Paul Popper/Popperfoto), 35 (Frank Scherschel/Time & Life Pictures), 36 (Roger Viollet),
37 (Popperfoto).
Shutterstock: 25 (Anyka).
TopFoto: 16 (The Granger Collection).
US Army: 13.
US Department of Defense: 21 (Weintraub), 30.
US National Archives: 17 (Army Signal Corps Collection).

Cover pictures:
Foreground: Members of an American landing party help their comrades ashore from a life
raft after their landing craft was sunk by enemy action on D-Day, 6 June 1944.
Background: US troops land with supplies and equipment on the Normandy beaches the day
after D-Day.

Every attempt has been made to clear copyright. Should there be any inadvertent omission,
please apply to the publisher for rectification.

A CIP catalogue record for this book is available from the British Library.

Dewey Decimal Classification Number: 940.5'42142

ISBN 978 1 4451 0049 4

Printed in China

Franklin Watts is a division of Hachette Children's Books, an Hachette UK company.
www.hachette.co.uk

SL001441EN

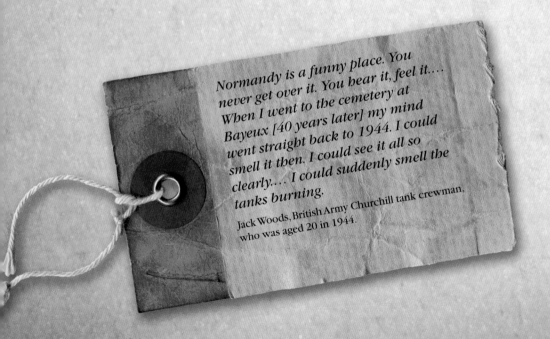

Normandy is a funny place. You never get over it. You hear it, feel it.... When I went to the cemetery at Bayeux [40 years later] my mind went straight back to 1944. I could smell it then. I could see it all so clearly.... I could suddenly smell the tanks burning.

Jack Woods, British Army Churchill tank crewman, who was aged 20 in 1944.

CONTENTS

A NIGHT OF WAITING

O n 5 June 1944, a vast army waited in southern England. Its mission: to invade and liberate Nazi-occupied France. The operation's code name was Overlord.

For weeks, every road in southern England had been jammed with trucks, every train packed with troops and tanks. A total of 300,000 Allied soldiers waited for the invasion to begin, but with the English Channel lashed by storms, 'D-Day' – the date set for the invasion – was postponed. The soldiers waited, joking to hide how nervous they felt, cleaning weapons, writing letters home. Most were scared.

They would have to cross 130 kilometres of sea, to land on five beaches in Normandy in Nazi-occupied France. Guarding those beaches was the German army, 'the most professionally skilful army of all time' according to General Dwight D Eisenhower, the Allies' supreme commander. The general anxiously waited for the weather to break. 'At 3.30 our little camp was shaking and shuddering under a wind of almost hurricane proportions,' Eisenhower wrote. But then came good news: RAF Group-Captain James Stagg forecast 'a period of relatively good weather … probably 36 hours' by the following morning (6 June). Eisenhower made his decision: 'OK. Let's go.' On D- Day, the so-called 'Longest Day', the battles on the Normandy beaches would change the course of history.

As D-Day approached, every port in southern England was crowded with ships, vehicles and soldiers. These Americans are loading LSTs (Landing Ship Tanks) at Brixham in Devon.

2 PLANNING OVERLORD

World War II began in September 1939 when Adolf Hitler's Nazi Germany invaded Poland. Germany and its allies were known as the Axis powers. The countries that opposed them (including Britain, France and, later, the United States and the Soviet Union) were known as the Allies. By 1941 German forces had occupied most of Europe, bombed Britain and invaded the Soviet Union.

In December 1941 Japan attacked the US naval base at Pearl Harbor in Hawaii, prompting the United States to declare war on Japan. Germany and Japan then joined forces to fight the Allies. The United States'

entry into the war soon tipped the balance in the Allies' favour. Its factories began to produce guns, tanks, ships and planes in staggering quantities. By 1942 the Allies were winning in the Pacific and in North Africa. However, German armies still occupied most of Western Europe, and in Eastern Europe German and Soviet armies were locked in huge tank and air battles.

German soldiers inspect a captured Canadian Churchill tank, following the failed attack on Dieppe in August 1942. In the Dieppe raid the Allies suffered heavy losses, and learned lessons.

FACT FILE

The Dieppe raid

In August 1942 the Allies learned a costly lesson when 6,000 of their troops, with tanks, raided the French port of Dieppe. It was a disaster. About 1,000 soldiers, mostly Canadians, were killed, and 2,000 were taken prisoner. The Dieppe raid showed that a seaborne invasion of occupied France would not succeed without massive force, careful planning – and luck.

The 'big three' Allied war leaders (left to right: Stalin, Roosevelt, Churchill) meet at Tehran in Iran between 28 November and 1 December 1943. The Allies agreed plans for the invasion of Europe and the defeat of Nazi Germany.

Eisenhower's mission

On 15 January 1944, US General Dwight D Eisenhower, in command of Overlord, arrived in England. His invasion orders, given on 15 February, were clear:

You will enter the continent of Europe, and in conjunction with the other United Nations, undertake operations aimed at the heart of Germany and the destruction of her armed forces.

A second front

The Soviet people were suffering terribly. Their government urged the United States and Britain to open a second front in Western Europe to relieve some of the pressure on the Soviet army. The Americans were already fighting fierce battles in the Pacific against the Japanese, but agreed that the war in Europe must be won first. In early 1943 the Allies decided to invade Western Europe, forcing the Germans to fight on two fronts.

The 'big three' war leaders were Winston Churchill (Britain), Franklin D Roosevelt (United States), and Josef Stalin (the Soviet Union). They agreed that the invasion, code-named Overlord, would be launched in 1944. The plan was to transport an army by sea from England to France, defeat the German coastal defences and go on to liberate Western Europe.

The opening beach attacks, code-named Neptune, would spearhead the largest invasion in history, involving over 4,000 seacraft, 10,000 aircraft and more than 300,000 soldiers. Most of the soldiers would be American, British and Canadian, supported by forces from many other nations, including Australia, Czechoslovakia, Belgium, Denmark, France, Greece, Norway, the Netherlands, New Zealand and Poland.

General Eisenhower (known to friends as 'Ike') was made supreme commander of the Allied forces. After months of planning and study of intelligence reports from spy planes, code-breakers and secret agents, the landing place was chosen: the beaches of Normandy.

Deceiving the Germans

The German high command knew an invasion was coming, but didn't know where the Allies would land. They expected the Allies to choose the shortest route: Dover to Calais. In 1940 the Germans had planned to invade England across this strip of sea, only 35 kilometres wide. Their invasion, Operation Sealion, never took place. The German air force lost the Battle of Britain in 1940. Without control of the skies, no invasion army could cross the Channel.

To make the Germans think that Calais was their target, the Allies staged a deception strategy called Operation Fortitude.

US General George S Patton was named commander of a non-existent army 'training in Kent'. Dummy airfields and planes, inflatable tanks, false radio messages and fake fleets popping up on German radar all helped to keep the Germans believing that the invading force would land at Calais.

Why Normandy?

The leader of Nazi Germany, Adolf Hitler, suggested the Allies might attack Normandy. His generals were sceptical. Normandy was best known for apples, dairy farms, sandy beaches and medieval towns popular with pre-war tourists. The sea crossing from England took several hours, and Normandy was 240 kilometres from Paris. Calais was more logical. Yet for the Allies, Normandy

The sea route to Normandy was longer than the Dover-Calais crossing However, Calais was more strongly defended. Also, Normandy offered the invasion fleet five target beaches.

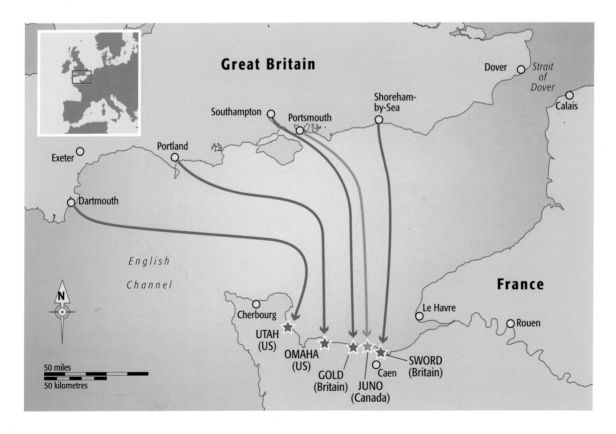

offered advantages. 'The defences [in Normandy] are relatively light, and the beaches of high-capacity and sheltered from the prevailing winds,' Allied intelligence reported in 1943. Normandy had a port, Cherbourg, and was within flying range for planes from English airfields. Landing there might catch the Germans off guard.

German soldiers man a defensive gun position on the Atlantic Wall. The Allies knew they had to smash through Hitler's coastal defences or lose the battle.

The plan

The Allied plan was to ship 39 divisions across the English Channel: 20 American, 14 British, three Canadian, one French and one Polish. In the first attacks, the Americans would land on two western beaches, code-named Omaha and Utah; the British and Canadians would land on three beaches to the east, code-named Gold, Juno and Sword. The German army was strong, but many of its best divisions were fighting in the Soviet Union, and others were scattered across France.

On D-Day (the first day of the invasion), Allied airborne troops would seize key bridges and stop German troops from reaching the beaches. The French Resistance (French groups fighting against the Nazi occupation of their country) would also hinder German counter-attacks by blowing up railways, cutting phone lines and attacking German columns on roads heading into Normandy. Once the Allies had gained the Normandy 'bridgehead', they would head east to Paris, and from there on to Germany.

FACT FILE

Fortress Europe?

To defend Nazi-occupied Europe, the Germans had built an 'Atlantic Wall' of coastal defences, from Norway to Spain. With 3,000 guns and millions of tons of steel and concrete, Hitler claimed his 'Fortress Europe' was impregnable.

US soldiers train on an English beach. This posed photo illustrates communication equipment, including a signal lamp and walkie-talkie radio, plus every soldier's essential survival trick – a 'foxhole' dug in the sand.

Preparations and training

In the weeks leading up to D-Day, southern England became an armed camp, as thousands of soldiers trained for the invasion. Backing them were sailors, aircrew, follow-up troops and support staff, and millions of civilian workers in Britain, the United States and other Allied nations. Work went on day and night to prepare the army. Roads and railways were busier than ever as troops moved to 24 departure ports along the English coast. Every soldier had been training for months – in landing craft at sea, attacking beach defences and climbing cliffs. Tank crews tried out DD (Duplex-Drive) tanks, designed to 'swim' ashore like boats: some of these new tanks sank, drowning their crews.

FACT FILE

Slapton Sands

In April 1943 US troops were training in landing ship tanks (LSTs) at Slapton Sands off the Devon coast. German E-boats (fast torpedo boats) made a sudden attack. Two LSTs were sunk and about 700 Americans were killed. The incident showed how D-Day might go badly wrong.

Reconnaissance

Information about the Normandy beaches piled up on the desks of Overlord planners. When the BBC asked radio listeners to send photos of the French coast, 30,000 letters with holiday snaps arrived the following day. Reports on beach defences came from the French Resistance and Allied agents in France. Allied special forces teams landed from submarines to check out each beach – even bringing back sand samples. Reconnaissance planes took aerial photos. A 3-D model of the beaches was constructed on the floor of St Paul's School in London for planners to study.

Ready for the off

By the first week of June 1944, most Allied soldiers in England knew that D-Day must be soon. Training had finished and soldiers were shut in their camps. Hundreds of planes stood ready. Warships were at sea. Every port along the south coast was crammed with transport ships and smaller landing craft, loaded with tanks, guns and trucks. By 5 June thousands of soldiers were aboard the transport ships, trying to to find space for all their battle kit. General Eisenhower warned them: 'Your task will not be an easy one. Your enemy is well-trained, well-equipped and battle hardened…' But, he insisted '…we will accept nothing less than full victory.'

Strengthening defences

In readiness for the invasion, the Germans strengthened their Atlantic Wall defences in France, covering beaches with obstacles and mines. However, the two top generals in Normandy disagreed over tactics.

VOICES

Confusion

Aboard the USS *Carroll*, hours before D-Day, Brigadier-General Norman 'Dutch' Cota (US Army 29th Division) warned his men:

You're going to find confusion … people are going to be landed in the wrong place. Some won't be landed at all.

General Eisenhower chats with US airborne troops before take-off. The soldiers are camouflaged (with cocoa powder and linseed oil) for a night drop inland from the Normandy beaches.

Gerd von Runstedt thought that German tanks should not be risked too early in the battle; Erwin Rommel believed in all-out attack – the battle would be won or lost on the beaches.

3

D-DAY DAWN

Hundreds of gliders towed across the Channel by 'tug' planes carried more airborne troops. This D-Day photo shows Waco gliders of the US 9th Air Force landing in Normandy.

FACT FILE

Jumping into battle

Paratroopers carried 32 kilograms of equipment, as well as their parachute. US airborne gear included an M1 rifle and bayonet, pistol, ammunition, grenades, knife, flares, rope, rations for 48 hours (including chocolate and water purifying tablets), first-aid kit, two pairs of socks and clean underwear.

By sunset on 5 June, England's southern ports were deserted. The invasion fleet was at sea. Deception tricks were still keeping the Germans guessing. A phantom fleet was apparently making for Calais; Allied planes were dropping metal foil, and ships were towing balloons to fool German radar. The Allies jammed German radio to prevent German pilots from reporting sightings of the Overlord fleet steaming through the night.

Aerial attack

Just after midnight on 6 June, the airborne assault began. Thousands of parachutes opened in the night skies over Normandy, and hundreds of gliders (the largest carrying 40 soldiers) were released by towing planes. In night battles, the British 6th Airborne Division captured river and canal bridges near the city of Caen.

Probably the first German soldier to die on D-Day was Helmut Romer (17), killed at around 12.15 am as British glider troops took the Orne Bridge.

Between 1.30 and 2.30 am, US 82nd and 101st Airborne paratroops landed behind Utah Beach. High winds, German gunfire and pilot error caused many soldiers to land a long way off target. Lost in the darkness, they used small metal devices called clickers (or crickets) to signal friends. One click was answered by two. No clicks meant 'shoot first'.

A group of 82nd Airborne landed in the town of Sainte-Mère-Eglise. A house was on fire, and the town square was full of people – German soldiers shot some paratroopers before they even landed. Private John Steele slid down the church roof and dangled from his parachute lines above the square until the Germans took him prisoner. A model of a US paratrooper now hangs in the same place as a memorial to Steele and his comrades. By 4.30 am the Americans had control of the town and its crossroads.

VOICES

One of the lucky ones

Paratrooper Robert Flory jumped with the US 101st Airborne, the 'Screaming Eagles'. He recalled:

The sky was being criss-crossed with tracer bullets and flak [anti aircraft fire]. I looked down and immediately went into a state of shock…. I landed in water up to my chest. I was in a salt marsh.

Flory waded to dry land. Many soldiers drowned, weighed down by their kit.

To honour the Allied airborne forces, a model of a US paratrooper dangles from the church steeple in Sainte-Mère-Eglise – as Private John Steele did on 6 June 1944.

Taken by surprise

German intelligence failed to give warning of the impending invasion. Few German planes were flying over the Channel, German radar stations had been bombed, and most German spies in Britain had been captured. Even when they picked up BBC messages in code to alert the French Resistance, the Germans took no notice. Why would the Allies be stupid enough to announce the invasion over the radio? Confident that the bad weather would delay any invasion attempt, the Germans had relaxed. Rommel had gone home to Germany for his wife's 50th birthday.

On the beaches nothing stirred save the wind and waves. Major Werner Pluskat, a German gun commander, checked his section of Omaha Beach at 12.30 am: sea rough; no ships. At about 1.00 am, German army headquarters in Normandy received reports of airborne landings. Was this the invasion, or a trick? At 4.00 am, German soldiers rushed off to fight 'parachutists' but found only dummies ('Ruperts'). Allied special forces soldiers ('Jedburghs') caused more confusion, setting off explosions behind German lines.

FACT FILE

The invasion fleet

672 naval ships and over 4,000 landing craft took part in the beach landings. Many of the troops went ashore in LCVPs (Landing Craft Vehicle Personnel), known to Americans as 'Higgins boats', each carrying 20 to 30 men. Other craft included the LCA (Landing Craft Assault), LCT (Landing Craft Tank) and LST (Landing Ship Tank).

This is the hour

At around 5.00, as it grew light, Major Pluskat looked out to sea again. What he saw sent him running to radio German army headquarters: 'There must be ten thousand ships out there. It's unbelievable, fantastic.' It was an amazing spectacle: a sea filled with ships. Then the thunderous noise of explosions began. Bombs from planes, battleship guns firing.

Allied warships pounded German targets along the coast before the invasion troops landed. This photo was taken on a US coast guard vessel close to the beaches as its guns went into action.

'This is the day … and this is the hour,' reported the BBC's Colin Wills, a war correspondent. 'The sea is a glittering mass of silver, with all these craft of every kind … and the great battleships in the background blazing away at the shore'. More than 4,000 landing craft began racing for the beaches. Most of the soldiers inside the small boats felt so seasick they just wanted to get to dry land, Germans or no Germans.

At 8.00 am, the BBC reported that Allied paratroopers had landed in France. By 10.00 am, Rommel's car was speeding back to Normandy. In Germany, no one had yet dared wake Adolf Hitler to tell him the bad news.

US infantry wait for their landing craft ramp to drop down as they approach Omaha Beach. For a few more seconds the men have some shelter from German gunfire.

VOICES

Part of history

I had the feeling we were part of a big chunk of history. Out of the window, there were planes in every direction and, below, hundreds of ships.

George Rosie, paratrooper with the US 101st Airborne, captured soon after he landed.

17

4 BATTLE FOR THE BEACHES

For the infantry of the US 4th Division, D-Day began at 3.30 am, as they scrambled in the darkness down nets slung along the sides of their ships and tumbled into their landing craft. The sea was rough, and it took three hours to reach the beach. US soldier Corporal Willard Coonen remembered it only too well: 'I don't believe anyone in the history of mankind ever got any sicker than we did'.

Utah Beach

Utah Beach was flat, with low sand dunes and a sea wall, behind which lay flooded fields (part of the German defences) and the small towns of Sainte Mère-Eglise, Sainte Marie-du-Mont and Carentan. The Germans had not finished all the defences, and the 709th Fortress Division, guarding Utah, included not-so-fit men in their 30s and others not fully trained.

Wading ashore on Utah Beach: many soldiers were soaked by spray before their landing craft hit the beaches. As they landed, they were trying to keep weapons and equipment dry, and avoid being hit by enemy fire.

Allied soldiers inspect a German beach weapon that didn't really work. These radio-controlled mini tanks were meant to blow up landing craft and vehicles, but few hit their targets.

VOICES

The benefits of training

Our gas-operated M-1 rifles became jammed on the beach with sand. We field-stripped [took them apart] and cleaned them in record time. We had been trained to do this blindfolded.

Sergeant John de Vink, US 4th Infantry

The US landing veered off-course. Brigadier-General Theodore Roosevelt Jr (son of former US president 'Teddy' Roosevelt) saw that the first landing craft was being carried 1.6 kilometres south of their intended target by the tide. He decided to carry on, saying: 'We'll start the war from right here'. It was a good move: the German defences were even weaker here, and by 7.30 am, battered by Allied bombs and gunfire, Utah's defenders had surrendered.

US Army Private Lindley Higgins waded ashore safely. He was then ordered to lie flat on the sand. This somehow set off his life jacket, which started to inflate. Thrashing around like a stranded turtle, he stabbed it with his bayonet to let out the air, then dashed up the beach. By mid-morning, the US infantry were off Utah Beach and had linked up with US paratroopers inland. By noon, army engineers were laying a temporary airstrip, and by dusk, 23,000 men and 1,700 vehicles were ashore. Casualties on Utah were light: 197 dead, and 60 'missing, presumed drowned'.

Omaha Beach

Pre-war photos of Omaha Beach show a quiet seaside scene: on D-Day Omaha became a bloody killing ground. Here the landing almost failed.

Behind Omaha Beach lay the villages of Vierville, Saint-Laurent and Colleville, linked by a coast road and seawall. By the summer of 1944, the crescent-shaped beach, almost six kilometres long, bristled with obstacles designed to wreck landing craft and tanks, many of them booby-trapped with mines. The US troops had to cross the sand, scramble up a shingle bank, then scale cliffs 30 metres high with just five exit gullies, all covered by German guns.

Things went wrong from the start. In thick cloud, pilots could not see the target. Most of their bombs overshot the beach and fell on farmland or in the sea. So did many of the 10,000 rockets and 600 shells fired from the ships. Defending Omaha were front-line German soldiers, tougher than regular coastal defence units. The US landing, timed for 6.30 am, ran late as landing craft came in slowly from 19 kilometres out. In heavy seas, ten craft sank, along with 26 heavy guns loaded on DUKWs (amphibious trucks), and 27 out of 32 DD (amphibious) tanks.

FACT FILE

Code letters
The Allied commanders gave each section of beach a code letter. On Omaha, the sections were A to G: Able, Baker, Charlie, Dog, Easy, George. Able was next to Utah. To the east, next to George, was Gold Beach.

Slaughter ground

Seasick and soaking wet, US infantry waded ashore into murderous fire from German machine guns. Many men were killed within seconds of landing. German soldier Hein Severloh recalled: 'The GIs tried to find cover behind the beach obstacles … or corpses of their fallen comrades… Often we could only see their heads and their

At Omaha, soldiers had to crawl through waves and beach obstacles to reach the sand. Wood and steel defences built by the Germans provided the only shelter from close-range enemy fire.

helmets.' The official US War Department account describes how some men jumped from landing craft ramps and drowned, dragged down by their equipment. Some men reached the beach but went back into the water for shelter or to help wounded comrades. Others crawled forward with the tide.

The rising tide covered the beach; staying put was not an option. 'There are two kinds of people are going to stay on this beach, the dead and those who are going to die. Now let's get the hell out of here!' shouted Colonel George Taylor, rallying his men. Soldiers ran forward, and in fierce battles,

one by one, German guns fell silent. By midnight the Americans were clinging on to Omaha, but at a terrible cost: 2,000 men lay dead on the beach.

VOICES

The shortest path

You knew the shortest path was a straight one, right across the beach. You'd hear zip zip, just strings of machine-gun bullets and automatic weapons … you'd run on a dry piece of sand and then hit water, and immediately tumble, get up, and keep going.

Captain Richard Merrill, 2nd Battalion US Rangers

American soldiers help injured comrades from the water after their landing craft was sunk by enemy gunfire. There were many acts of heroism on Omaha Beach that day.

Gold Beach

Gold and Sword beaches were the targets for the British landings. In between was Juno Beach, where the Canadians came ashore. Gold Beach was about eight kilometres long, with the town of Arromanches at its western end. Flat and sandy, the beach was enclosed by low cliffs, where the Germans had big guns. First, Allied ships pounded the gun sites. Then, at 7.25 am, the landing craft raced on to the shore. The waves were too rough for the amphibious tanks, so the landing craft came into the shallows to offload the troops. On Gold Beach Sergeant-Major Stan Hollis won the only Victoria Cross awarded on D-Day. He attacked a German pillbox, taking 25 Germans prisoner; later, he charged a machine-gun post and drew enemy fire to save two comrades.

Commandante Philippe Kieffer, a Free French army officer, led commandos on Sword Beach. For the French, victory on D-Day also meant seeing homes and villages destroyed.

FACT FILE

Ground won

By nightfall, 25,000 men had landed on Gold, and held 13 square kilometres of France. The 20,000 Allied troops on Sword had control of a slightly larger area. On Juno, 21,000 men got ashore and some were already 11 kilometres inland, within sight of the city of Caen.

Sword Beach

Sword was a similar length to Gold Beach, lying between Lion-sur-Mer and Caen's port of Ouistreham. It had fewer German defenders than expected, yet still only 24 out of 40 tanks landed safely. Among the first ashore were Free French Commandos led by Philippe Kieffer, who would later become one of the first French soldiers to enter Paris. British Commandos were piped up Sword Beach by Bill Millin, one of the few pipers to play during a World War II battle. The tide rose so high that the beach shrank to just nine metres wide. As Millin stepped off the

Canadian troops wade ashore on Juno Beach, carrying bicycles. The bikes were meant to provide faster mobility on land, but many were soon abandoned.

landing craft ramp, he and his bagpipes toppled backwards into deep water. 'Luckily someone pulled me upright,' he recalled. Sword became a huge traffic jam of men and vehicles, and as the soldiers hurried inland, they saw a brave French girl on the beach, helping the wounded.

Juno Beach

The Canadians landed on Juno – five kilometres of beach between La Rivière and Saint Aubin. They had a tough time: 20 of the first 24 landing craft were lost, and 34 out of 40 Centaur tanks sank. On landing, many soldiers were hit by German machine-gun fire. The high tide hid booby-trapped 'hedgehogs' – metal pyramids with mines, which were much more difficult to make

VOICES

Landing on Juno

The last thing I saw before I ducked my head was one of the craft to our left blown sky high. A few seconds later we felt the scrape as the craft struck the sandy beach … and we were leaping into the foam.

Don Doner, Queen's Own Rifles Regiment (Canada)

safe when submerged. On Juno, the Canadians suffered over 1,200 killed and wounded, but by evening they were making good progress inland.

23

As D-Day dawn approached and the massive guns of the battleships began to pound the shore, Allied midget submarines surfaced stealthily off Normandy. Their job was to guide tanks and landing craft onto the beaches. Some submarines had been submerged for up to 48 hours – an uncomfortable wait for crews squashed inside a boat just 15 metres long.

All kinds of vehicles

Peering from their beach defences – concrete bunkers, pillboxes and gun-positions – German soldiers were astonished to see Allied tanks rumbling out of the sea. The DD 'swimming' tank had two propellers and was kept afloat by a canvas 'skirt'. Many tanks sank before reaching the beaches, but those that made it were quickly into battle. More reliable was the DUKW 'swimming truck'. The Allies also landed specialized vehicles such as armoured bulldozers, bridge-laying tanks and armoured tank-recovery vehicles to tow wrecked tanks out of the way. The Allies' best tank was the US Sherman, but it was outgunned by the German Tiger. A 57-tonne monster, the Tiger's 88-millimetre gun could 'knock out' a Sherman at 4,000 metres.

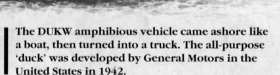

The DUKW amphibious vehicle came ashore like a boat, then turned into a truck. The all-purpose 'duck' was developed by General Motors in the United States in 1942.

FACT FILE

Hobart's Funnies

Major General Percy Hobart's engineers designed some unusual D-Day machines, jokingly called 'Hobart's Funnies'. The Bobbin tank unrolled a canvas strip to make a road; Crocodile tanks carried flamethrowers; Petards lobbed mortar bombs at concrete bunkers; and Crab tanks used flailing chains to explode mines and clear a safe path through minefields.

Weapons and equipment

The Germans had formidable smaller weapons, too: the Panzerfaust ('tank fist') anti-tank weapon; the Nebelwerfer ('smoke launcher') rocket launcher; and the MG 42 machine gun, which could fire 1,400 bullets a minute. Most infantry soldiers on both sides were armed with rifles and semi-automatic carbines.

To scale the Normandy cliffs, Allied Commandos and US Rangers had trained with rocket-launched grapnel hooks fastened to long ropes, and ladders – some borrowed from the London Fire Brigade. The 'rocket grapnel' was fired up towards the clifftop where the hook was supposed to find purchase, but on D-Day many ropes were so wet and heavy that the grapnels fell short. Under fire, the men had to scramble up as best they could.

VOICES

Landing on Sword

Bombardier Norman Marshall, a British Commando, drove a DD 'swimming' tank onto Sword Beach:

With a terrific crash we hit the sandy bottom, there was no flood of water in the tank, no panicky screams from the crew, and I knew that we were okay for now. All I could see through my periscope was blue-greenish water with thousands of bubbles rising upwards.

A German gun battery at Longues-sur-Mer, between Omaha and Gold beaches. The concrete still bears shell marks from Allied naval guns on D-Day.

Air power

On D-Day, the Allies had more than 11,000 planes to fight the air war over France. By contrast, the Luftwaffe (German air force), after suffering weeks of attacks by Allied bombers, was short of planes, fuel and pilots. In June 1944 the Luftwaffe had, on paper, over 220 fighter planes in Normandy. However, only 158 of these were ready for combat. Altogether, the once invincible Luftwaffe had only 300 aircraft to send into battle on D-Day.

Even worse was the shortage of men to fly them: the Luftwaffe was losing 400 pilots a month fighting on two fronts against Allied aircraft. The handful of Me 109 and Fw 190 fighters was no match for the swarms of Allied fighters: British Spitfires, Mosquitoes and Typhoons, and US Mustangs, Lightnings and Thunderbolts. German soldiers looked in vain for their own planes. They joked bitterly: 'if it's silver, it's American; if it's blue, it's British; if it's invisible, it's ours'.

FACT FILE

Aerial assistance

Air power helped win the battle of the beaches. During June 1944 the Allies flew about 90,000 air missions – more than in any other month of the war. Allied Army Engineers built ten airstrips in Normandy in the four weeks after D-Day.

The crew of a USAAF B-24 Liberator bomber on an airfield in England, ready for their next mission over occupied France. Air bombing was a key part of the Allies' D-Day strategy.

B-26 Marauder bombers head for Normandy. All Allied planes were painted with D-Day stripes on their wings, for identification. These B-26s dropped smoke-bombs to screen the Allied landings.

Destruction from the air

In the weeks before D-Day, Allied planes bombed French towns, roads and railways. On one night – 21 May – 129 French rail locomotives were destroyed by British and US bombers. On D-Day itself, bombers pounded German airfields and beach defences, while hundreds of fighters flew above the invasion fleet. As the Germans tried to move their army towards the beach battles, they were attacked by Allied fighter-bombers, which shot at and bombed any vehicle that moved by day, including trains and columns of trucks, tanks and horse-drawn wagons. German tanks could therefore only move after dark. Many ran out of petrol. Soldiers ran out of ammunition. Each counter-attack was immediately smashed by Allied planes. Only bad weather kept the Allied pilots away.

The sight of so many friendly aircraft, with their distinctive 'D-Day stripes' on the wings, cheered troops on the Normandy

VOICES

Corridor

New Zealand fighter pilot John Houlton shot down the first German aircraft on D-Day. He explained:

We were told there was a corridor across the Channel.... Our night fighters were patrolling on either side, and were likely to regard any plane that was found outside the designated area as hostile.

beaches. With so many planes in a small area, however, there was a risk of being accidentally shot at or bombed by your own side. Sadly, this did happen. Allied planes attacked Allied troops, and Allied soldiers and ships fired at their own planes – victims of the confusion of war.

27

6. THE NEXT STAGES

By the afternoon of D-Day, Allied troops had 'dug in' on the beaches. More men and vehicles were landing all the time, at times turning the beaches into a military traffic jam. Of the five beaches, Omaha was by far the most precarious. Many American soldiers were digging foxholes in the sand to shelter from German gunfire.

As ships unloaded more troops and supplies, the beaches became crowded. This photo of Omaha shows barrage balloons, flown to stop low-level attacks by German planes.

FACT FILE

Bloody Omaha

The Americans lost 2,000 men on Omaha Beach – more Allied casualties than the other four Normandy beaches put together. One small US town – Bedford, Virginia – lost 23 young men on 'Bloody Omaha'.

US Rangers with German prisoners after the capture of Pointe du Hoc. This photo of the shattered enemy strongpoint on 8 June shows Lieutenant Colonel Rudder's HQ, with the US flag proclaiming victory.

Attack on Pointe du Hoc

US Rangers were given a special mission: to climb the cliffs and destroy German guns at the western end of Omaha Beach, known as Pointe du Hoc. The Rangers headed for the wrong (eastern) cliff by mistake and lost three landing craft in the rough seas. They struggled ashore 450 metres east of their target. Their DUKWs, which were carrying climbing ladders, got stuck in shell holes on the beach. The Rangers had to make a dangerous ascent of the cliff without the ladders, while Germans shot at them and tossed down grenades. When they finally reached the top, the Rangers found no guns, just telegraph poles.

The Rangers' commander, Lieutenant Colonel James E Rudder, led his men inland. One of them was Sergeant Leonard Lomell: 'We didn't stop; we played it just like a football game, charging hard and low. We went into the shell craters for protection … if the fire lifted, we were out of that crater and into the next one.' Lomell and his friend, Sergeant Jack Kuhn, found the missing guns in an orchard, and the Rangers put them out of action with grenades. They then fought German soldiers all the following day, until on 8 June fresh troops came up from Omaha Beach. By then, more than half the 225 Rangers had been killed or wounded.

The news spreads

Gradually, news of the landings seeped out. In Germany, Hitler was hopeful of victory: 'Now we have them [the Allies] where we can destroy them,' he crowed. The Allies must be driven back quickly; the invasion 'must last no longer than a day or so, a week at most'. 'A great test of strength has begun,' blared the Nazi newspaper, *Volkischer Beobachter*, reporting on the battle in Normandy.

Troops move inland from Omaha. Reinforcements poured in as the Allies consolidated their hold on the coast and began the liberation of France.

On the afternoon of 6 June, Prime Minister Winston Churchill told the House of Commons in London: 'the first of the series of landings in force upon the European continent has taken place … everything is proceeding according to plan. And what a plan! This vast operation is undoubtedly the most complicated and difficult that has ever taken place.' On hearing this, German generals were worried. Did Churchill's use of the word 'series' mean that other landings were imminent?

The landings continue

As Churchill spoke, German hopes of victory on the beaches were fading. Allied troops were ashore on all five beaches in Normandy, and more were constantly arriving. The first troops had to get off the beaches so that the next wave of soldiers could land. Tanks and infantry began to

VOICES

A mighty endeavour

In a 'radio prayer' on D-Day, President Franklin Roosevelt told Americans:

Our sons, pride of our nation, this day have set upon a mighty endeavour; a struggle to preserve our republic, our religion and our civilization, and to set free a suffering humanity.

move inland, turning the invasion force into an army of liberation. For many young Allied soldiers, D-Day had been their first experience of action. They had watched friends getting killed and wounded. Moving inland, they saw dead Germans too. One dead German soldier, surprised by the early morning invasion, still had shaving cream on his face.

Darkness did not fall until after 10.00 pm, but on the beaches black smoke from burning vehicles had blotted out the sky well before then. Many of the invasion troops were desperately tired, but few had any chance of rest. Some soldiers dozed in foxholes in the sand. Others found shelter behind walls or hedges, to snatch a meal and a drink.

'Beachmasters' worked all night to control and direct incoming troops and vehicles. Tanks and DUKWs churned up the sand. Medics attended the wounded, evacuating the most serious cases to ships returning to England. Teams of soldiers began the task of removing and identifying the dead.

FACT FILE

The Sherman

The US M4 Sherman tank was the Allies' best all-round tank. Originally developed in 1941, the Sherman had a top speed of 45 km/h, a 75-mm turret gun and front armour 85 mm thick. Tough and reliable, the Sherman's main weakness was its tendency to catch fire when hit.

Advance towards Caen

The Allies planned to link up the five beaches, to establish a 'bridgehead'. The invaders would join up with airborne forces inland, and capture key French towns. The first targets were the city of Caen and the port of Cherbourg.

Off the beaches, Normandy's narrow country lanes and high hedges slowed the advance of tanks and other armoured vehicles.

VOICES

Crash, crash, crash

British gunnery officer Captain Bryan Dodsworth drove a jeep inland. His job was to direct gunfire from battleships by radio. As 'friendly' shells burst all around, he dived for cover. His diary notes read:

Grovel in the bottom of a trench … crash, crash, crash, one after the other.… Heaven knows how near they [the shells] are … have ceased to care … get up very shaken indeed.

He survived, and died in 2009, aged 89.

Canadians from Juno Beach could see Caen, and hopes were high of a speedy success. During the afternoon British Commandos captured a canal crossing called Pegasus Bridge and met up with airborne troops, close to Caen. However, the advance was then halted by a determined German defence.

The Normandy countryside, or *bocage*, was an ancient landscape of small fields, high hedges and steep ditches, making it very hazardous for an advancing army. Hedges gave cover to enemy snipers and held up tanks. Sergeant Curtis G Culin came up with a solution: he and his men welded saw-teeth onto the front of a tank. Nicknamed a 'Rhino', the hedge-destroyer could chop through the thickest hedge.

The German situation

The German army in Normandy was far smaller than the one fighting in the Soviet Union (59 divisions compared to 165). It had 1,500 tanks and many soldiers with years of battle experience, but a large number of the units were half-strength. Guns were low on ammunition, tanks and trucks were short of petrol, and hundreds of horses were used for hauling guns and wagons.

Nevertheless, many German soldiers hoped the battle could still be won with Hitler's promised 'revenge weapons'.

British infantry move cautiously through a field near Caen. Allied soldiers quickly learned that the Normandy countryside could hold unexpected dangers, such as hidden German snipers.

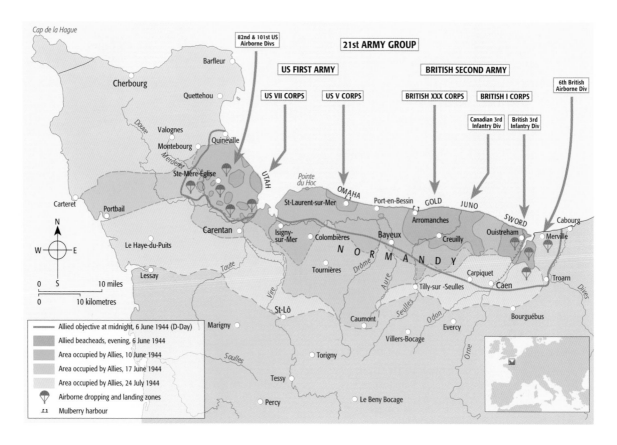

A map showing the progress of the invasion during June–July 1944. As soon as the five beaches were linked, the Allies began advancing inland.

German propaganda told Allied soldiers they were trapped on the beaches, while 'flying bombs' would soon unleash death across England, destroying their homes and the bases from which the Allies had sailed.

Objectives achieved

On 7 June, known as D+1, ships steamed across the Channel bringing more troops to the beaches of Normandy. A total of 65,000 men and 19,000 vehicles left the English ports of Weymouth and Portland. On D+2, US forces from Omaha met up with the British from Gold Beach. On D+6 (12 June) US soldiers from Omaha and Utah made contact. When all five landing beaches were joined, General Eisenhower could breathe a small sigh of relief.

FACT FILE

Hitler's 'revenge weapons'

The first V-1 flying bomb was launched against England on 13 June 1944. This stubby-winged pilotless plane flew at almost 800 kilometres per hour and had a range of 360 kilometres. Once over the target, its jet engine stopped and it dived to explode. During the following months, 3,500 V-1s killed over 6,000 people and injured 42,000 more in southern England. The V-1 was followed, in August 1944, by the V-2 rocket – so fast it was impossible to shoot down.

In the first week after D-Day, 330,000 men and 50,000 vehicles were put ashore. By the end of June, the Allies had landed more than 500,000 men, 148,000 vehicles and 570,000 tons of supplies, including 60 million ration cartons for soldiers. Fuel cans piled up in fields in stacks as high as houses. Mounds of artillery shells lined country lanes, while ammunition boxes were everywhere – a machine gunner could fire 20,000 rounds in a few minutes.

Storm clouds gather

Success was not yet assured, however. The Germans were massing troops and tanks, and they began firing V-1 flying bombs at southern England from launch sites in northern France. Also, the weather was worsening. Until the Allies could capture Cherbourg, they had no French port, so it was vital to bring in artificial harbours, known as Mulberries. Two were towed in sections from England.

By 18 June the Mulberries were assembled off Omaha and Gold Beaches. On 19 June a fierce storm hit the Channel, and for the next three days waves pounded the beaches. The Mulberry at Omaha was wrecked, and the one at Gold was damaged. Before the storm, 34,000 troops had been landing every day; after the storm, the Allies managed only 10,000 a day – until the Gold Beach Mulberry was repaired.

Eisenhower warned the US government that 'the going is extremely tough'. He gave three reasons: the Normandy countryside; the weather; and the German army. The Germans were, indeed, trying their best to counter-attack, transporting soldiers and tanks across France, even from the Eastern Front, to join the battle. But the German army was short of fuel, food and bullets, and many of its soldiers were exhausted.

FACT FILE

The Mulberry Harbours

The two Mulberries contained a million tonnes of concrete and 70,000 tonnes of steel. Each had 213 sections, the biggest being 61 metres long and weighing 6,000 tonnes. The harbours were towed across the Channel to Normandy by 150 tugs. Designed to last 100 days, the remains of the Gold Beach Mulberry at Arromanches have survived for over 65 years.

A giant section of Mulberry Harbour on its way to Normandy. One of the artificial harbours was wrecked, but the other survived to help ensure the Allies' success.

The after-effects of the severe Channel storm that hit on 19 June 1944. The beaches were littered with battered and half-sunk ships. The flow of Allied reinforcements was cut until the damaged Mulberry at Gold was repaired.

7 LIBERATION BEGINS

D-Day brought the start of liberation for France and the French people – but also more hardship and suffering. The invasion turned Normandy into a battlefield. Dead horses and burned-out vehicles blocked the country lanes. Dead cattle lay in the fields. Houses were shattered by bombs and shells. Most French families remained in their homes. As Allied troops tramped through battered villages, men, women and children came out to greet them, offering flowers and wine to celebrate liberation from the German occupation, which had begun with France's defeat in 1940.

Americans hand out gifts of chocolate and chewing gum to enthusiastic French children. Liberation was at last becoming reality.

VOICES

A warm welcome

A Canadian Army officer enjoyed his liberation welcome in the French city of Rouen:

Everyone seems to be in the street, and no one ever seems to be tired of waving to the troops passing in their vehicles, who likewise never tire of waving back ... the children yell and wave flags ... and the Army rolls through.

The price of victory

The first French town to be liberated was Bayeux on D+1 (7 June). Liberation, however, came at a high cost. The Allies bombed Cherbourg before fighting their way into the port on 27 June. The Germans blew up much of the harbour. Caen also suffered. On 6 July the Allies sent in waves of bombers, starting fires that burned for 11 days. By 10 July, Caen (where William the Conqueror lay buried) was free but in ruins; 3,000 French people had been killed.

The Allies learned day by day that the German army could still put up a fight, even when running short of tanks and petrol. Fuel for the Allies' tanks, trucks and planes came in by ship, and by August through an undersea pipeline that pumped 4.5 million litres of oil per day across the Channel from England.

Hitler intervenes

The German army's commander, Field Marshal Wilhelm Keitel, phoned from Berlin on 10 June to ask Rundstedt what he thought they should do. 'Make peace, you fool,' retorted Runstedt, who was convinced that German troops must pull back to defend the Fatherland (Germany). Hitler was enraged. 'Every man will fight and fall where he stands,' he insisted, and Runstedt was dismissed. Rommel fought on until 17 July, when he was badly wounded in an air attack on his car and was forced to leave Normandy.

Caen was left in ruins by Allied bombing. Little of the old city remained. It was not fully rebuilt until 1962.

FACT FILE

Undersea pipeline

PLUTO, the 'Pipeline Under The Ocean', carried fuel oil from England to France. A steel pipe, 7.5 centimetres in diameter, it was laid by ships and barges on the Channel's seabed. Pumping stations in England were disguised as bungalows, garages and teashops.

Within days of the Normandy landings, many German soldiers knew they were losing. They did not have enough tanks, planes or troops to hold on to western France. Yet some of the best German troops were still not in the battle – they had been ordered by Hitler to hunt down the French Resistance instead. Small groups of resistance fighters, armed by parachute drops from the Allies, were attacking roads, railways and bridges across France. The Germans retaliated savagely by shooting and hanging civilians.

Hitler told Günther von Kluge, his new commander in the West, to hurl the Allies back into the sea. Hastily assembled counter-attacks in early August were crushed as Allied aircraft bombed and rocketed German tanks and troop-carrying vehicles. When Kluge ordered a retreat, he was immediately replaced by Field Marshal Walter Model.

The Falaise Pocket

By mid-August, General Patton's US 3rd Army was moving rapidly outwards from Normandy, overrunning the retreating German forces. At the same time, Field Marshal Bernard Law Montgomery's British, Canadian and Polish armies pushed on past Caen. The Germans tried to counter-attack, driving deep into Allied lines, but this left them in an exposed position. Allied commanders immediately took advantage, trapping 100,000 German soldiers in what became known as the Falaise Pocket. Hemmed in

VOICES

What a slaughter

Sergeant Mackenzie of the British Royal Engineers saw the remains of the German 7th Army in the Falaise Pocket.

What a slaughter. Nothing but Jerries [Germans] and tanks and vehicles and guns all smashed up.

This map shows the Allies' 'breakout' from the beaches and their advance through northern France. More Allied forces landed in the south of France on 15 August 1944 (Operation Dragoon).

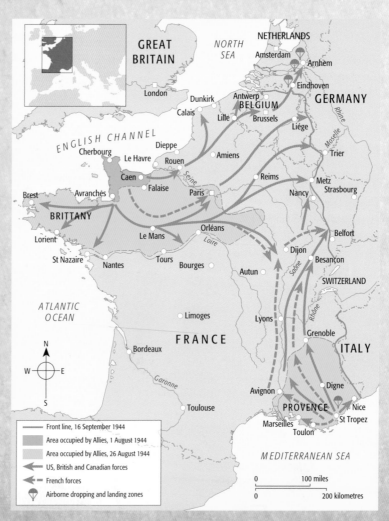

by Allied armies on three sides, the Germans' last narrowing escape route east became known as the 'corridor of death'. Tanks and trucks ran out of fuel and had to be abandoned. Allied planes harried the retreating Germans, and many thousands of soldiers were killed or taken prisoner.

Victory in France

With the German army in France broken, the Battle of Normandy was over. On 19 August the people of Paris rose in revolt against their German masters, who abandoned the city, and on 25 August Allied troops entered Paris. Overlord had achieved its first objective: the liberation of France. It had come at a high cost, with 14,000 French civilians killed and tens of thousands wounded, and 500,000 buildings destroyed or badly damaged.

Paris was liberated on 25 August 1944. Free French soldiers paraded through the Arc de Triomphe to celebrate the end of Nazi occupation.

FACT FILE

The Battle for Normandy

German casualties in Normandy were over 60,000 killed (some estimates are much higher) and 180,000 wounded. More than 200,000 Germans were taken prisoner. During the 11-week battle, nearly 40,000 Allied soldiers were killed and over 160,000 were wounded.

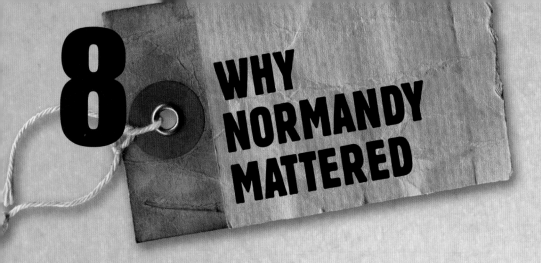

8. WHY NORMANDY MATTERED

The D-Day invasion was a turning point in World War II. To many Germans, it showed the war was lost – defeat was now just a matter of time. General Eisenhower reported thankfully that 'the German army in the West has suffered a signal defeat.' Operation Overlord was, indeed, a catastrophe for Germany, already enduring terrible losses at the hands of the Soviet armies in the east.

Prior to Overlord, some in the German camp had entertained hopes of making peace with Britain and the United States to prevent Germany from being overwhelmed. The Normandy beach landings on D-Day destroyed all such hopes.

German losses

The D-Day battles destroyed 25 divisions of the German army and left 18 badly weakened. The manpower shortage was now so serious that boys as young as 16 were being sent into battle to replace older soldiers killed, wounded or captured.

The Germans also lost masses of equipment, including 1,300 tanks, 20,000 trucks, 3,500 aircraft and more than 2,000 big guns. Withdrawal from France also meant the loss of U-boat (submarine) bases

Thousands of German soldiers, captured on the invasion beaches, became prisoners of war. This group is waiting to be shipped across the Channel to internment camps in Britain.

FACT FILE

First fatalities

The first Allied soldier killed in battle on D-Day is thought to have been Lieutenant Den Brotheridge (British 6th Airborne) at the Orne Bridge, around 12.15 am. The first US fatality was Lieutenant Robert M Mathias, 82nd Airborne. He was hit by ground fire as he was about to parachute from a C-47 plane. He jumped, and his men found his body on the ground.

on the French coast and V-1 'flying bomb' launch sites. The Luftwaffe lost its French airfields from which it could launch attacks on Britain, and many of its remaining pilots.

Not even Germany's new 'wonder weapons' – jet fighters and V-2 rockets – could make up for these losses.

The end of the war

In three months (June–August 1944), the Allies swung events decisively their way, bringing the end of the war closer. By September 1944 the Allied armies had crossed the River Rhine into Germany, and by spring 1945 they were moving into Berlin. Hitler killed himself on 30 April, and on 8 May 1945 Germany surrendered. The war was over in Europe. By August 1945 the Pacific War was over too.

VOICES

Lucky to survive

Royal Navy gunner Lol Buxton was on the British destroyer HMS *Goathland*, which was in action off Sword Beach on 5–6 June 1944:

I shall never forget what I saw and experienced that day. It was absolute hell.... We were lucky to survive. Every time I return to Normandy, I know what a fantastic feeling it is to be alive.

By May 1945 the war in Europe was over and people celebrated VE Day (Victory in Europe). This was Wall Street in New York City. The crowd's joy was shared all around the world.

> Visiting a D-Day memorial or war cemetery is a moving experience. The graves and lists of names remind us of the thousands who gave their lives in 1944, in hope of a better future for humanity.

D-Day remembered

D-Day was an historic battle. It was an endeavour that united men and women from many nations in a common cause. The beaches on which it was fought have become places of pilgrimage. Every year veterans return to Normandy, though as time goes on their numbers have dwindled. Most of those who visit now are too young to remember the war, but many find the Normandy beaches a moving experience. The flags of the nations whose soldiers fought on the Allied side fly in French towns along the coast. Visitors can see the beaches and the remains of German defences, tanks and the Mulberry harbour. There are museums and a number of impressive memorials.

There are immaculately maintained war cemeteries across Normandy: two American, 16 British, two Canadian, one Polish, one French and five German. The Normandy National American Cemetery at Colleville-Saint-Laurent contains over 1,000 graves of soldiers killed on D-Day. Many more US soldiers' bodies were taken home for burial in the United States after the war.

Making history

Each survivor of D-Day had a story to tell. There were many examples of individual heroism, of people helping one another, of bravery in the face of appalling dangers, of bad luck and good fortune. Each soldier, sailor and airman helped to make history. They were assisted by millions of civilians from several Allied nations, who provided crucial support for the operation. D-Day succeeded because many nations, great and small, worked and fought together. In so doing, they helped to inspire the ideal of the United Nations, the organization set up after the war to promote world peace and international cooperation.

On 6 June 1944 people in many countries celebrated the news of D-Day. For millions in occupied Europe, D-Day meant hope that liberation was a step closer. That is why the Normandy beaches remain special. The soldiers who landed there, many of whom gave their lives, helped to end Nazi tyranny. Their victory gave hope that Europe would again be free, and a world at peace might emerge from the ruins of a world at war.

FACT FILE

Those who did not return

On D-Day the Allies suffered about 10,000 killed and wounded; the Germans had between 4,000 and 9,000 casualties. At the Normandy National American Cemetery, 38 pairs of brothers are buried. Among them are Preston and Robert Niland. The Nilands' story inspired the 1998 film *Saving Private Ryan*, which recreated the Omaha Beach landings.

GLOSSARY

Allies The alliance of Britain, Australia, the Soviet Union, the United States and other nations that fought against the Axis powers (chiefly Germany, Italy and Japan) in World War II; also known as the United Nations.

amphibious Describes a vehicle that can travel on water and land.

artillery Large guns that fire explosive shells.

Axis powers The alliance of Germany, Italy, Japan and other nations that fought against the Allies in World War II.

Battle of Britain The air battle between the British and German air forces that was fought in the summer of 1940.

battleship A very large warship with big guns.

bayonet A stabbing knife fitted to a rifle.

carbine A rifle-type gun with an automatic loading mechanism and short range.

column A long line of soldiers and vehicles on the move.

division A large army unit of about 15,000 soldiers.

DUKW An amphibious vehicle that could travel on water or on land.

field marshal An officer holding the highest rank in the British and German armies.

fighter-bomber A fast fighter plane, adapted to carry bombs and rockets.

Free French French forces who fought on the side of the Allies after the defeat of France in 1940.

front An area where opposing armies are facing each other or where fighting between armies takes place.

general An officer in command of an army: the highest rank in the US Army.

GI 'General Issue', the nickname for an American soldier.

grapnel A hooked anchor on the end of a long rope, used for climbing.

grenade A small bomb that is usually thrown, but can also be fired from a rifle.

infantry Soldiers who fight on foot.

intelligence Information about secret plans and activities, especially those of the enemy.

jeep A small US military vehicle.

landing craft A low, open, flat-bottomed boat designed for landing troops and equipment on shore from a ship.

mine An explosive device that can be hidden in the soil or underwater.

mortar A weapon that lobs an explosive shell high in the air to fall on the enemy.

Nazi A member of Adolf Hitler's National Socialist German Workers' (Nazi) party, which ruled Germany from 1933 to 1945.

pillbox A concrete, box-shaped defensive structure, with slits for soldiers inside to fire through.

propaganda Information and publicity put out by a government to promote a policy, idea or cause.

ramp A hinged door on a landing craft that can be lowered to allow troops to disembark.

reconnaissance Observation of enemy positions.

resistance Organized groups who fight against an occupying enemy.

sniper An army marksman who fires a rifle, usually from a hidden position.

special forces A force of soldiers who carry out secret missions, often behind enemy lines.

SS The SS (German for *Schutzstaffel* or 'protection squad') were a special Nazi armed force known for their brutality.

tracer bullets Bullets that glow, showing a gunner where a stream of bullets is aimed.

Victoria Cross The highest award for valour that can be given to members of the British armed forces.

Waffen SS The Waffen ('fighting') SS was an elite force of German soldiers.

war correspondent A journalist reporting on a war. In World War II war correspondents reported news from the battle zones for newspapers, magazines, radio and cinema newsreels.

FURTHER INFORMATION

MUSEUMS

In Normandy, there are museums at many key sites, including:

- Airborne Museum, Sainte-Mère-Eglise
- Arromanches D-Day Landing Museum
- Battle of Normandy Museum, Bayeux
- Memorial Museum, Caen
- Omaha Beach Memorial Museum at St Laurent-sur-Mer
- Rangers Museum at Grandcamp-Maisy

There are also museums devoted to D-Day in Britain and the United States:

- D-Day Landing Beach Museum, New Orleans, USA
- D-Day Museum, Portsmouth, UK
- National D-Day Memorial Foundation, Virginia, USA

BOOKS

Days That Shook The World: D-Day by Sean Sheehan (Wayland, 2003)

Graphic History: The Tide Turns: D-Day Invasion by Dan Abnett, Doug Murray, Richard Elson and Anthony Williams (Osprey, 2007)

My Story: D-Day by Bryan Perrett (Scholastic, 2004)

Usborne True Stories: True Stories of D-Day by Henry Brook (Usborne, 2007)

Visiting the Past: D-Day Landings by Bob Rees (Heinemann Library, 2002)

WEBSITES

www.bbc.co.uk/history/worldwars/wwtwo
This BBC website contains resources about World War II, including a special section on D-Day and Operation Overlord.

www.dday.co.uk
A website dedicated to those who took part in the D-Day landings.

www.iwm.org.uk
The website of the Imperial War Museum, London, includes information on D-Day.

www.pbs.org/wgbh/amex/dday
A PBS website containing lots of information and resources about D-Day.

INDEX

Page numbers in **bold** refer to pictures.